The Monastery of Stars

The Monastery of Stars

Poems by

Shaun T. Griffin

Cover by Shay Culligan

Cover art by Ismael García Santillanes

ISBN: 978-1-950462-55-1

Kelsay Books Inc.

kelsaybooks.com

502 S 1040 E, A119
American Fork, Utah 84003

Todos los días el mundo muere.
Todos los días nace.
—*Octavio Paz*

for my family—

Debby, Nevada and Brenna, Cody and Suzette

Acknowledgments

The author is grateful to the following publishers for permission to reprint the following poems, some of which appeared in a slightly different form:

High Desert Journal: "Last Night in San Jose"

Red Rock Review: "Songbird, Seamstress of the Broken Note," "Two Hawks on the Freeway to San Gabriel," and "Stooped to the Landlord Earth"

Cutthroat: "These Are Old Windows," "The Labyrinth of a Mind," and "Sleeping on the *Terraza* Without You"

Brilliant Corners: "The Night Hayden Carruth Listened In at the 1836 Opera House, Johnson, Vermont"

An Amazing Eclectic Anthology: "Monument of What Is Not Seen," "Muir Trail Ranch, in the Shadow of Mount Shinn," and "When, for One Morning, Touch"

Broadside by Black Rock Press: "Songbird, Seamstress of the Broken Note"

The Limberlost Review: "Letter to Doug from the Base of Teton Pass"

Common Ground Review: "My Brother, Afloat at Sea"

San Pedro River Review: "Ode to Love in the Nursing Home"

The Fourth River: "Prison Chronicles: Volunteer Training," and "Pictures of Ayre"

Contents

I

Learning to Polish Razor Wire—Elegy for Bobby Gonzales

You lie face up in the obituary
like an owl with no moon to wing by,
the dirge of Alzheimer's finally slowed.
For twenty years you wrote poems
in the workshop—small, cryptic
epigrams to the past—the scar
laced throughout—and we listened,
not knowing how to intercede
save their passage to the page.

Bobby, you should never have died
in prison. Granted immediate pardon,
the pernicious suffered you into their arms
and now we imitate death's smirk:
how could a state spin your life
into three lines in the bottom
of the local paper? Do not try to answer—
you, replete with the chaplain's calm
and Vietnam Vet ball cap, you who

could not countenance grief on a yard
where grief plays its sporadic opera.
Do not, Bobby, say why the knife
bloodied the hand—say only
you forgive the legal ruminations,
the allegation of hope where none
should persist, and choose, instead,
to write poems to the God that
would not lay down in this place.

Letter to an Unfinished Father

Now that you have left
        there is nothing to rebuke
                your broken gait—and if I

could wrest from you,
        temptation to spin the halls
                of some other mind—yes

I would lie in your path
        like gravel—and still, the robes
                that fascinate

will clear your closet: tomorrow
        you might be Lear,
                by Sunday the storm from which

he sings. This is what we have:
        the skeleton of good-bye—
                the final séance

into which we drift
        to believe your words
                as they eddy from the pay phone

in Georgia, in Jupiter,
        in our every day of
                the furious, bloated telegrams

to no one, as even we
        who start this letter,
                can no longer listen.

Now That I Have Been Stilled by the Breath of Starlings

and the chime is moving to early wind,
I can almost believe the day has begun:

these hours spent on the porch to dig
my heels into earth, wrinkle the nose
in lavender after the long dissection

of work, for mine is not a labor of hands,
but of calloused arteries.
Yesterday, in the unglowing office,

my colleague upright before me
to unravel the fear of funders—
and failure
touched our names like widows
in their grief.

The melancholy of making good
has many coordinates

but I step between them to find my perch
is missing
from who I was, exempt
from understanding—hod carrier with a mortar

of no wall but the fallen. This is how
a dozen starlings
become my wind sock

for the muffle of the human voice,
a susurration of notes
                    and something more

these many birds sing upon me.

Songbird, Seamstress of the Broken Note

for R. H.

                                        Yesterday
a friend cried the news into the phone—
she had gone—the auburn hair—
                        the robin

who made art
                seem like a window
                        we could open
                                and share.

All March the robins have been in the trees—
and their call is bright, original—
                a melodic dance
                        of throat and body.
This is how she worked—
                and when I heard
                        its searing pleasure
I knew something of creation.

How is it a woman
                sings in our midst
to herald the dawn of art
as if it were the first brush on canvas, the first
                                tremble of feet
across the stage?

                This is what the robin
                            did for me
                and what I will know of her
short time here: that art,
however misunderstood and maligned,
                            returns

at the end of the fallen day
                                     to startle
us from sleep. Robin of the pre-dawn hour—
                  come to me now.

The Bog Road to Roundstone

Somewhere in the blue and heather horizon,
wind like a flag from no country of man,
and she, the one I have pedaled with
all these, our thirty-plus years, the sheep

running before us to the edge of land,
we turn to the ocean, a lone bicycle
in the mist of centuries, and slow, up the hill
to the bridge that became us—what we crossed

to arrive this fortnight of moons in tandem,
but more, in the hope of coming to the other side—
that when we stop, just now in the heat
of this autumnal equinox we share with the pansies

and asters hung from the café window,
the wind and stone of each, our separate lives.

The Night Hayden Carruth Listened in at the 1836 Opera House, Johnson, Vermont

when so many friends were in the room—
        and his words echoed from the balcony of cold
starlight, what each one said at the podium—
           Hayden, I loved you, man

        from three men and a woman—
and Hewitt ran the lightning chorus of Johnny Spain's Heifer
to the roof beams, and Budbill summoned the wail

        of Bechet and Webster but not before
beauty leapt from her cage in Wormser's hands—
        and over in the wooden chair, *la femme* Carruth rose to
        pluck
        the late notes of *Brothers*—when hippest Hayden
     sang
for all of us—

        well it might have blown down in Johnson fog,
the smoke of his voice to save a note of freedom
and responsibility, a last riff for the poets who stomped
        the makeshift pews,

          Hayden, it was you up
        there,
sweatin' and bringin' the four walls close to the breath of need and
     hurt—
     when they dove into the inexpressible art
        of a man who would not go down without the
    ecstasy

        of peace,
        "the great pain assuaged."

Two Hawks on the Freeway to San Gabriel

for Stephen Shu-Ning Liu

On this white morning of so many silences—

    when I think all faces have disappeared—
you return, thinned by age and what
      passes for silence,
      but your shutter snaps bird after bird,

and when I read your poems
          into the microphone, you fly
    ten thousand miles to Fuling,
          bird of no country,
    to report on family
      living in the ashes of disbelief.

    How do I see you now,
          your daughters like herons
    and their daughters, trailing behind
this homecoming without a home?

After two decades of wandering
    you chose the desert, and now,
        in retirement, must choose again—
    a city of last resort or burden of no sound?

    Slight nomad of the creosote bush,
      do you wade the moon's darkness
for all of them? My friend, is there a word
        for what cannot be said
    when the hawk returns

to its kin over the strange freeway below?

Letter to Paulann at Los Prietos

Of William Stafford's seven decades
on this earth, she scoops from the patina

of his pacifist years, hands cupped
to remember the poet in the pre-dawn hour:

smoke from a woodstove, the early foment
of words to paper, how he sat before the face

of Dorothy, and then, off to work in the oaks,
digging footpaths in the Santa Barbara hills.

This is how he resisted the urge
to fight, what he did with the soil,

scrub jays, and chaparral. All this effort
to be alone with thought like prayer—

that she releases in a letter
to my own desert—so far from peace,

from any hint of release, now that the war
is done and the broken soldiers return

to scuff the story of their lives,
these voices in the dust held out to me.

Waiting to Be Chosen

Girl without words in the library,
       you sit with five students at the table,

choose a stanza from "Up-Hill,"

Christina Rossetti's poem about the long
       walk from home. When I call on you,

there is nothing to share,
       the empty vowels
           are dust in your mouth.

You stammer, "I can't read,"
       shoot the words through the stacks,

like the mystery of flight
       from your absent father.
       Is there any mouth

to recall what the poet would have said,

       any servant to enter your eyes
and claim a young woman?
Not in this small town.

"It's nothing. I'm over it," you confide
       to the shelves. On the way out,

the teacher whispers, "The family's a mess,"
as if you disappeared from the room.

Now you cannot trust the poem
       to be shared. You must pretend
to understand it has left without you.

Pictures of Ayre

Frame One
    Ayre is a woman
    who walks the road edge.

Frame Two
    She stoops in the mountain sun
    to inhabit her bones.

Frame Three
    She pushes a baby carriage to town—
    the tourists have no fear—it is only Ayre.

Frame Four
    Ayre lives in a crude shack hidden from view—
    except to those who think Ayre is everywhere.

Frame Five
    Ayre wears tennis shoes, two blankets,
    a cap and sunglasses in any weather. They mask her skin.

Frame Six
    People mistake her for a stone or a stump
    when she sits on the road.

Frame Seven
    Ayre is like someone who breathes
    but cannot exhale.

Frame Eight
    Ayre is a dream that wants shelter,
    hot food, a bath—but the dream persists without her.

Frame Nine
>She is the background, the distance,
>a leaf before she flies off the road.

Frame Last
>Walking through two winters and summers
>she cannot begin to live inside.

Mother

I watched you burn the light of six lives—
dancer, painter, Percival's sister—
in an armchair at eighty-seven
as we moved you to an elder home.

After thirty-two years of teaching,
you swung the blackboard to greet us—
there was no chalk to write your name.
The vowels on the board fell to dust,

and even though they wanted to erase
the powder, you waited for the next door
to open, to enter with your Gauguin
in the rose garden. I remember

a mother strong: Old Gold cigarette,
martini, and bridge, remember the screen
door slamming to work—where the
farmworker kids thought you mother, too—

and my father, alone in his Irish lair,
could not breach the day without you.
At El Adobe, we ate below the black
and white still of the brittle Nixons,

their red leather chairs almost surreal
above the former Capistrano jail.
This is how we lift the dust, how we
push ourselves away. As we leave,

you dance in the waning sun of your
window, of the roses that remain—
vigilant, hybrid, storytellers
who blush in the flourish of day's end.

Leaf Fall in the Voting Booth

for Brenna

It seems, as no thing has seemed,
leaf fall attenuates
the venal glow of this time:

down-canyon through
red-orange and sienna,
bark tracks and river eddies

to root silence, refuge
of dissolution, beneath a moon
of wind and freeze drop,

the percussive refrain against
the leaves—*let go,*
let go, give chlorophyll

to earth, what will be wrested
from the dormant veins
to foment in stagnation:

the untimely ruin of a star
and solitary flower
on so small a stone as this.

A Reluctant Fog

presses up the valley
into the wet snow of daylight.
Audrie cries into phone:
Chip is gone.

I cannot forget
the June day she stepped into the yard with him,
balloons on the fence, to have his first

meal outside of prison
in a dozen years. My dog and sons
were abundant in their not knowing
who ate at our table.

II.

When the two of them
left for Utah I imagined a great highway of loving
touch, unlike any in his small room.
But I was not privy

to the gun held
at his shame.

When he fell from
the Vegas bar to the sandstone walls
of Carson, he lay beneath the hills of
sage and smoke on the yard.

Sometimes the stones
stampeded, witness to the memory
of a species in denim.

III.

My friend,
I cannot let you into this moist earth
like a wound that opens, cannot let you walk
from these arms.

At first, you never got out,
and then when you did, the stones returned
to your feet, each step a cavalcade
of memory and dream,

to slough their refuge
from your spine.

And your poems
and stories? You wrote nothing down
for fear it would be broken. A storm before
the gate closed behind.

On the Fiftieth Anniversary of the Arts Council

I.

In the slow autumn of a life, rain
clouds halting too, little remains

save the ancestors' artifacts. A mystery
of misgiving must not portend:

last night, after weeks of trying, the sky
opened to an image of the Stone Mother

whose extant beauty intoxicates.
But how does its luscious color explain?

A reluctant gift turns again
to remind: art requires no answer.

II.

In this dry land, rain reconciles
a past of extraction. For wind

and others who need this place,
it is sustenance for the ideal.

Art's rudimentary hand
in the petroglyphs

is our hand, a remembrance
of stone on this anniversary

of creation—the runic elders
who left their prints on us.

Prison Chronicles: Volunteer Training

I.

Some hope of decay
may return to this room
before it's over,
but I cannot imagine a light
to redeem the red rock
at Stewart Indian School.

We sit in rows
below the tattoo gun collage,
the poster of inky biceps,
and wait for instruction.
At mid-morning, the veteran
of Rahway, Rikers, and 9-11

tells us *he feels safest inside.*
He must have lost his trademark scowl—
when the gates close
on any man, it is fear
that fills his mortal stem.
Later he asks if we *like it*—

the training, that is,
because we won't
get these four hours back.

II.

Last night a twenty-nine-year alum
of my poetry class called.
He too is afraid the gates
of the free world will close
and he will once again shudder inside.

For whom does poetry
account? On the list
of do-gooders, poetry is left
off the slide. Maybe poems
belong among the contraband?

III.

I try not to believe
the token wisdom he passes out,
try to instill hunger
in the flesh of men
who no longer need
hunger. And the poem, the word

takes its own form,
but today the prison seems
little more than sleep—
a sentence for the guard
and volunteer alike.

IV.

How is it we choose
this army of regret
and make room for its stanzas?
I am certain his pain—
very real from the blown heater pipe
they beat him with—has nothing

to do with learning. And I pray
the poems will return
when I begin again in September.
But they may not.
Already, I have been told
it is too dangerous to volunteer.

Monument of What Is not Seen

The desert is wet, the air scented
                     with moisture's frail cloth.
A tumbleweed mocks thirst
          and for the first time in months,
the alkaline lake bed paddles to life.

There is a bone of man
                 below its white horizon—
every song before another man
           came to this place murmurs beneath.
The days stalk the rib cage of the deceased
          like two crows in the salt brush.

Some torment of desire
                wakes to cloud sun
and make-believe spring this late July.
           That it happens once every decade
is immaterial. For now, the desert
              is a prayer of flight.

In the distance, smoke clears
          to announce: this is the itinerant
home of water—breathe in,
               swallow, turn your feet to its cave,
come down to the insurrection.

Muir Trail Ranch, in the Shadow of Mount Shinn

Crossing Paiute Creek to the hot springs,
two deer in the meadow, our feet
cold in the stones of rushing water. My son,
his oldest and first friend, sink to their waists
in the hot mud. The reeds tease us
to dreamfulness. I think of those before—

the man for whom this place was named
and the ghosts of those who age in stone:
the rucksack, the burn of nightfall mosquito
on the trailhead of yellow bricks.
A blue Venus crawls over two conical peaks—
there is no wind to send the mind to sleep.

At dawn, pine needles float in the coffee
and the moon steps away. Halfway to ten,
I set off for the Florence Lake Ferry,
the boys scavenge my pack and I empty
the flask, a cairn on the granite below.
I track their boot prints in the dust:

eight days to ascend the back of Whitney
before work rubs time extinct. This trail
I nearly died on before they were born—
a river of snow that becomes the trout
in their hands and somewhere, a fire
skips into the monastery of stars.

When, for One Morning, Touch

Days that I slip from the warm earth
      of your hands and drive thirty miles
into the eastern sky of sage and dust,
      for those who monthly meet

to pick up the broken skin of us,
      nurses, cops, mothers, and farmers—
I come again to you, old friends, pressed
      to the rudimentary palms of flesh, of one

person without the dawn, to redress desire:
      as if touch were an element from which
the atom of attraction sprung,
      not physical, but the organic compound

of freedom, a periodic table of inclusion
      when our voices collide with the ancestral voice
that will not go unheeded, and
      this motionless morning finally relents.

Last Night in San Jose

All day the swifts came to the balcony
and disappeared in the river wood.
We sat below them, quick to the wings

that whipped and fell in the midday heat.

My son was at the desk corralling numbers,
and his bride at hers, concluded she must wait:
the country below kills its strangers.

We are like swifts, close to this ridge

of cloud and mountain without a sign
to follow, darting for a respite from hunger,
for the sudden eclipse of need in the sky.

And then these birds become black flowers
in the rain. Cut from flight for a second,
they circle the ones we love in the humid air—

then home to the ribs of water and wood.

Letter to Michael from the Enterprise Library on East Shelbourne Avenue in Las Vegas Where I Closed *Raising Wild*

I

How does the sun arch its back
among these spines that crowd the aisles,
and there, a dictionary splayed like a great
horned owl, to read the definition of *afflatus*:

divine breath of knowledge.
And when I reached the solemn passage,
the close of night that led me outside,
it was breath from the northern desert of home—

this tumbler of stones, stars, and
wind you polished for your children
who disappear on the ridgeline.

II

Once in the Andes, I saw a condor—
miles from earth, whose wings were canyons,
and it circled the massive peak, but I could not soar,
left on a path to watch. He took me as passenger,

bird of many stories, and then I remember
the warmth outside the library—the gift
of your waterless journey, how two girls
appeared on the horizon, and for a minute,

flew with them until they were gone.

Trying to Say Something about the Empty Poetry

A tryst with the reader

A mystery of dormant detours

An anecdote of moons

A form of restraint

A balloon of no color

A sorrow of springs

A way to feel without feeling

And then a way to feel again, the empty

A loss inside the eye

A tomb for nothing and then

A tomb for the saturation of effect.

Elegy for a Mountain

They will not airbrush the mountain's flanks
back to their original, arboreal strength.
They will not sing what the dust says
when it blows over heads to the children below.
There is no alchemy to retrieve the gold
from its binary roots of profit and loss
when the skin of the mountain is removed.

This is an old story in the West: what steals
from the consequence of lives
in this community, broken by what has happened,
and aching still to banish the footsteps of greed.
All around, the trail of this mine
carves its presence and we, the itinerant ones,
extract what is left when they leave.

Penal: Love Song for Izzy

This is what pulls
        the throat from its bones—

when so many will be
        tried and convicted

and so few emerge
        from its deathly resolve:

if I wager my life
        you have a job.

Ode to Love in the Nursing Home

for Bill

All night the ambulatory faces tripped
to their rooms. Love did not speak

in that place. Love laid down
in the dining room, looked for

the automatic door, became
the thorn of disbelief. We ate

a burger, potatoes, and warm salad,
tried to swallow what was unsaid—

the presence of a person outside,
someone who needed you—

the last premonition coming to visit
before the surrender to stones.

Waking in the Scarlet Aviary

for Javier and Shelley

I.

All at once helicopters of orange, blue, and
        yellow arrive, dream-ships
               in the almond tree. Prehistoric feeders,

        the *lopas* caw and crack the pods
like kites on the leaf stems
        before the rage of sun returns.

Yesterday, a horrible clash of beaks and
        feathers; they were druids in the clouds,
            hot smoke above the shoreline.

          I make no promise to shroud the iguana,
the wasp hatch in the pool, the purple crab
        crawling from the loo. What begins as sonic

rapture ends in the burnt notes of jazz, and they
        lift from the carnal hunger,
           hooked in a filial arrow of flight.

II.

Inside, my wife is wracked with stomach cramps.
        She knows the in-laws will assuage: healer,
           homemaker, angel of the white sand,

        and he, architect of this house of birds—
who rises early to fly with them. They mistake two
      strangers for family, take us in, navigate

the skin of our rootless swagger. We are like these birds,
red-orange cranes of light: sudden, imminent,
boisterous—opposites the hands

who will quiet the knot of discomfort.
Our lives, drawn together like string
on this beach. We give them over to a separate

pleasure: because our children wed, we too
marry something feral, numinous
and scarlet like a bird of two countries.

Letter to Doug from the Base of Teton Pass

I

This morning I read of birds,
of their life-saving presence
to a human rights journalist.
Yesterday, Tu Fu's couplets hung
in this rarified air—and his
birds echo from history:
our work is not done, our lives
decorations on a mantel of small hope.
I write from this beautiful
place in the manner
of Tu Fu—to tell in plain song
of my error: the window seemed
large—I would see someone else.
I was wrong—it was not me,
only an illusion of greatness.
My work remains at home. I answer
you with humility now that I am
in the mountains and rivers
without noise. The osprey
reminds: the edge of tomorrow
waits, but I cannot turn from
today. Old friend,
I send this note to you
from afar: I fled my country
but return, alone, stripped
of possessions, happy to walk
this road. Thank you for the idea
of more—it is less I choose.

II

How does a life
funnel to this endless choice:
one bird, one path?
In the moonlight
I answer—not now, my friend:
too much remains
unfinished—this work of one life
consummated in labor.

It is not brown dirt
I turn over
but a dirt of souls
unearthed in the
landscape of home.

III

Outside, a moose
crowds the view;
inside this flesh, there are
no roads to dissect
but I cannot muffle the bird's cry.
Cry for us who become them,
I want to say.

What can we feign
to be alone in this private
sanctuary? I lie by Fish Creek
having pedaled the backside of Teton Pass,
Tu Fu in the flowers
waiting for the next millennium.

IV

I think back to the man
before this, remember
what I wanted
when nothing
but the words kept me,
and then the decades—
by this time, this river
that cannot be assuaged.
I answer with what I am
at its shore. It is enough
to be quiet, an egret,
and some would say art
of no consequence,
save the elegant wings
passing overhead.

V

So poor is my sight
the Szechuan businessman
stoops by Firehole River
to help me tie a fly. I think
of the master, bent in his age,
murmuring to the heron, blue-gray,
streamside, two old reeds
in the grass, no food or cover
to keep them, and in a fit
of reconciliation, drinks plum wine
and eyes the thin legs in water,
the girth of his days gone
to survival, the sum of effort

to wander with a bird
in the colony of little wind,
and this finally is what he frames
in ten thousand poems—
almost to the mountain hut of friends,
who wish for sleep against
the mat of stone. Just then
a raven crosses
the everlasting river
in the light of stars.

Bird That Could Not Right Itself

I

Bird that rose out of the onion field,
weighted with a rabbit, two crows
in chase, struggled to lift and
dropped the kill straight into her path.

She swerved to miss the flurry
of feathers, but the window blurred
into a still and unnatural shape.
She screamed as I folded its wings

in newsprint. It lunged to the road edge,
hung listlessly in barbed wire until
I freed its talon from the fence.
It struggled to fly again, spread

on the sandy rising, prostrate,
gasping, hunting my eyes, and I
left its storm of brown and white
to singe the hour goodbye.

II

A Paiute elder drove to retrieve it,
but what can be retrieved
that man has hushed? I thought
of Li Po in the moonlight, releasing

the egret from death's ivory shore.
I have no pretense to stand among them,
bird or poet, only the knowledge of bones
in my palms, the blue-green iris like

a delphinium on the desert floor.
Now the specter of regret
circles in mad flight—how could we
steer into such foreboding?

III

Against the boarded skies of Tonopah
we woke in the Mizpah, nomads
of no room, and wondered what had flown
to find us. I walked to the used

bookstore, found Delmore Schwartz—
imagined him at the hotel bar,
lonely, hiding from something. I walked
on to the meeting. Neither my wife

nor I could shake the bird. She asked why
it dropped the rabbit. It carried too much,
I said, and looked across the room
to all of us weighted with work.

On the road north we found him.
I laid him in a Mexican blanket
and drove the silence to home,
the onion field reddened with dusk.

Today I will name him—thorn bearer,
tree lion, but it will not be enough
to go down into the earth, in the grip
of hunger that will not cease to stare.

Forgetting Heaven

There are blows in life so hard I cannot know them—
—Cesar Vallejo

You sit in the hollow of your cave
to memorize lines from a past.
For twenty-nine years you were
Sherpa to the poem, but today
cannot lift its sound to your lips.

Your voice is mute as a moth,
a peripatetic thing, a mood
in the chapel. You post poems
to the heaven of forgetting,
and pray again they will return.

How is it a mind swims to the other
shore and leaves its lover behind?
It is only by force of mind
your poems came into the world—
and by force of loss, they retreat.

Bobby, the poem is idle, and you in a cell
dressed for Sunday visiting
that may or may not arrive. The ghost
of your crime has limped away
and the preacher's face may yet assuage.

Tomorrow and those to follow
hunt the man you are now—
but I remember when mind met mind.
The howl of life bones slip to sand.
Hold my hand, old friend, as we go down.

The Train to Ancona

A priest sits next to me on the train to Ancona.
Two days ago, a stranger led me to Lorca's grave.
At the headstone were the words
Lorca eran todos—
Lorca was all of us—like the priest
must believe of Christ.

This morning, atop King Emmanuel's bronze stallions
Rome disappeared in the clouds—
like we disappear on the tracks
through this valley. And yet,
the headstone and the priest
remain apart from time.

Where is the stranger who leads from here,
who will say what we know
of faith and bullets,
these islands strewn like litter
in the vineyard of unrest?
Where is the stranger?

In the Albayzín, a cloistered nun
opened a trap door
to give us *magdalenas*—small cookies.
We were admonished to answer
Sin pecado, concevido.
Without sin, I was conceived.

A young voice answered
the wooden dark.
From where did she arrive, on whose
camel was she draped
for the desert crossing? Surely the priest
was there, Lorca too. An Italian girl

smiles at my question
as she rises in the vineyard,
and the priest smiles, Lorca smiles,
but the train moves on
without death to pronounce her name
in the ribs of what is left behind.

Carruthian

I have said the word,
the word that cannot be said,
spoke the silence,
the silence that cannot be spoken,
opened the man,
the man that cannot be opened.
I have waited for his voice
to reverberate, to sing its throaty
song in these pages, and it may
yet sing—may yet move
one more reader—this poet
who lived without the solace of
easy comfort, this poet
who wrote lines to assuage
grief's angel, this poet
who made snow, loss, and wood
his friend, this poet who broke
kill frost with the silence of "North
Winter," this poet who wrote
the barbed silence
of "The Asylum," this poet whose
only wound was being alive
in the vast northern Vermont
mountains and waking to tell
the story of "cow-shit farmers,"
and the foot soldiers of its valleys. There
was no Carruth; there was
the eye, the hand, the polymath
mind, stubborn on the axe,
on the grinding wheel of Hudson
River quarterlies, and finally
the birth of blues in a poem.
There was a man who looked like
Hayden in the cowshed,

writing into the ash of dawn,
and slow, walking his dog to Johnson,
that woolen mill town of a few thousand
hard-working farmers,
those people for whom
he was witness to the story
of New England dropping down—
and yet, none of this
is the story, the "Paragraph,"
the dialogue of virtue
set against his long stride
into the unknown,
one hand against the storm
of this small, jazzed
planet, this bluesy ensemble
that had he a choice,
would have been his vinyl legacy,
not the books
that kept the man
from a shelf of isolation.

Sleeping on the *Terraza* Without You

For five nights you have risen beneath the canvas
and walked the tile fragments—your toes

on the miniature paintings,
and once you were a blackbird

in the grape trellis, spitting the blood
seeds into the white fan of daybreak,

each turn of sun almost insignificant
where sun has eaten from our lives

for two summers, and the honeysuckle
swallows the ribs of the guard rail without you—

woman who wears white and yellow
like a vine and cannot imagine this morning

without a crawl up the fence of home, miles and
miles to the west where blackbirds discovered land

and brought grapes to the rooftop
of two who cannot for long divide flesh

and become its tutor: the night has breached
and we do not believe the aberration

of one apart from this place you last rested
in the smoke and wind of every breath.

This Saturday When Nothing Came from the Week's Labor

Clouds, sun, thirty-eight degrees,
and the hammer of waiting tasks:
split the kindling, hang the Christmas lights,
and recite the sparrow's buzzy trill.

Reading Hall's essays on Pound I think
there is no mind to capture this light.
Even the *Cantos* left something unsaid.
If the mind's orators presume to know,

I choose the room of unknowing,
the everyday tumult that reveals
an echo of arrival in the chill wind,
how the sparrow insists daylight

bloom in tranquility. To the east,
the seven ranges of light
break across the Great Basin.
A bony locust bisects the mountains—

Dead Camel, Stillwater, Clan Alpine,
Fairview, Desatoya, Shoshone,
and Toiyabe. By sight's end
I have ridden these ridges

to their origins. The woodsmoke
portends: let light resume its work.
A white-crowned sparrow
distills the kill frost of morning.

II

Managua Diary

11/1

Left Los Angeles at midnight,
sunrise out the plane window—
café con leche in the only open bar.
I dodge customs with a three-hour wait—
San Salvador simmers in the foggy light.

Today I will listen to the tracks
of politics or fear. It will be translated
like a symbol of peace for the right
and the left. And the workers
will fly to their knees, pray

that someone dictate their silence
to the reporters. By noon I will find
a taxi to Managua and the driver
will tell me, stay low—*siempre abajo*—
and I will nod with a gringo twenty—

is there any other way to fly?

11/2

Here I am with my bootleg Spanish
talking to foot soldiers—
no blade for the recourse of the tongue.

11/4

No order to the day—
we arrive, we disperse like rain.
I reach for a fallen bougainvillea—
Isabel blooms in the taxi.

11/5

The earth rises—
a temblor at dawn.
I wake in a dream of furious shaking—
God at the end of my bed.

Outside, God is at the end of the street—
billboards proclaim Christianity,
Socialism, and Solidarity—these three
for the common good. A pink sign
in the sky—pink with blood of Ortega's
roses—but could it be papaya
or hibiscus or the perfect calm of sunrise?

In the market I paint a street vender.
He is twelve, his brother six. Together
they proclaim innocence, then hunger—
the alchemy of dirt and water
below the festive signs that need
an occasional boy selling trinkets for food.

I call the cousin of a woman
who knew my son. She works for
the most powerful senator of my home.
Her cousin flies the banana streets

to study for school. What will I say—
an oxcart slides between us—
two children and some green wood
wobble the Central American highway.

We have touched plant, kitten, baby,
and a centipede that rivals a scorpion—
felt the rise of cement beneath our feet.
Yesterday, in the coffee *finca,* a tree
old enough to remember the last sign
in the sky—was it my party or yours?—
these leaves in brown hands surrounded by us.

At the lake, the prints of first man
in volcanic ash—six thousand years
to reveal our footsteps. In that time
we have walked to the school, the library,
the altar, and the cemetery. But something
is awry. The smell of what we love—
all that we love decomposes
on lips, eyebrows, earlobes—maps
to the corner of desire.

11/8

Right and wrong are not tourists here,
but they have been fattened
on the harvest of bones.

11/11

José Angel, our driver, left home
at twelve—his father bruised the boy
to the street. He pulls to the stop—
a child juggles balls for *córdobas*—
out the window, a mother of fifteen
rides the curb, her baby strung
between young trees in the hammock.

Every day this taxi arrives
to ferry us, welcome strangers,
through the knock of stone streets.
Yesterday we ate *gallo pinto,* drank
leche agria—Isabel despised it.
We hear stories in the taxi—
this is a permanent condition.

We hear words like social order,
civil society, and the rule of law—
cognates to devour a wretched
leader. At the next light, a boy
flipping balls—Isabel lowers
the window and Socorro cries—*!Ten cuidado!*

The shelter of two *córdobas*
will not keep him from the stones
at his feet. His mother will ask
for the money and he may run
like José Angel. He may disappear
to a river far from here. When the rains
come late in the day, the window

closes and the river swells. If he is
swimming, there might be cover—
he may become part of a picture
in a new room. At dawn, José Angel
has a breakfast of fried onions
and chicken—*fuerte*—to deliver
us from the ghost of what remains.

11/14

The last night in the green sky.
At the airport Claudia squeals "Wow"
like she is making love. I hug Julia,
a baby who flew into my arms. Isabel

tries to explain, but the new ones
in the taxi reel at the pink signs. José Angel
pleads for a poem—I have none.

The grackle sleeps in the canyon
of small eyes. At the light, a girl
tosses balls on her brother's shoulders—
until our presence kills her labor.

Tomorrow I leave the hot leaf
that has become my home.
I will try to immigrate, forget
the measure of a hand held by a street.

11/15

In the dark the grackles—*zanates*—
wake the trees. The jugglers
have gone home. No one
hears José Angel and me
try to say—*hasta pronto*—until…when—
tomorrow, the next tomorrow,
the next election? There is no
exact translation for leaving a man,
a country, no precise word to cut
rider from driver at the curb.

At six o'clock I will descend
to snow—Managua a silhouette
of last birds in the red sky.
The day will end as it began:
we will disappear like clouds.
José Angel will park the taxi,
put his swollen eyes to bed,
our paths diverted from what
we almost said before dust and rain
sutured the light of day.

12/8

I woke José Angel last night—
what darkness will greet this cable
to the green island? Socorro
writes from the stone kitchen—
her daughter Julia kissed the envelope.

Today, the doubtful work
of making tools for the hands
that stir in opposition.
The daughters of American Aid
ask how we scab the country

with clever lines to redeem
a century of banana thievery?
No place to ordain the fellowship
of *taxistas,* but José Angel
drives out of history to mail three cards,

black and white stills of children
before they juggled the cross hairs
of traffic, before the last pony
rode in and promised calm
in the city close to the water.

12/19

Claudia says, "I didn't know they killed
sociologists—" no breath at the border
for her friend from college. This is
where the book closes—the chapter
on leading a revolution.

Her soft tissue will write it,
the testimony of a woman in this barbed world.

These tiny cables from Managua—
high-wire messages that sting the ear.
Claudia's voice fades to snow. It is
the winter solstice and a lunar eclipse—
the first in three hundred seventy-two years.

Perhaps Ortega played with the light
at the other end of the globe,
perhaps the tinsel on the tree
flew to clouds we cannot see,
perhaps the thorns of her friend's shadow

pierced the moon.
Perhaps it was a candle of pink
lit on her behalf—perhaps Claudia shot
the moon full of obsidian arrowheads
so we would stop looking for light.

And perhaps the jugglers stooped,
trying to find their balls
in the ashen orb. No, I think,
it was none of these—just the steps
of soldiers marching across the moon.

Stooped to the Landlord Earth

for friends reading Cry the Beloved Country

All day I thought of you, lying
in the beloved country of Alan Paton.

In the cross of my small town
I shuttled a woman and her daughter

to shelter, poked the bags for food
and clothes in the country she cried home.

In the echo of the bar her daughter
almost looked dry. I heard the book

drive its wedge. My friends,
I would have joined you to read,

but the scent of fear sent them walking.
I grew restless, knew the dollar

would pound itself to rent,
and out of this hardscrabble day,

emerge the moon, she and her
daughter drew down to rest.

Driving to the Arts Council Meeting

for Doug

Driving west on Flamingo, I imagine you
chasing the sorrow of seven day's teaching,
ponytail fanned to Syracuse or beyond

all literary confusion in the marrow
of a body rent with Argentine resolve—
the bloom of faces in the rampant blush

of this new Las Vegas morning, the first
rain in a city that never drives wet
except of course on cocktail napkins

in the blood dark of strip joints
and nameless taxi rides to the desert's
eternal womb—oh how do you forgive them,

their teacher who wanted this hour
to pace the parapet of his office,
reading to no one in the wet palm sky?

Ode to the Colombian Journalist Selling Time-Shares in Orlando

Periodista, your microphone is a wand
to distract tourists from time saved
in the water lily hotel where you dispatch
news of the front to bromeliads
loved by your brother, the bohemian poet
who reaches from the kingdom of coca
castled by soldiers where no immigrant
slips from view to report on the grave
condition of falling to exile, and tourists
funnel to the closer, sharp with his tie
and grin like an exotic moth who rents
the canopy of ease that she may thrill
to the replica of life before dissent.

Among the Monarchs with Marien

This June morning beyond the gorge
of tongue and country, I drive her

to the airport where, huddled
in the froth of hands that led to high school

in the American sage and stone,
the runway lights lift her eyes

through the borders of bone and corn
to a village of sisters in the mosquito wet.

Like Lawrence in a field of sun and Indians,
she flies to the green coast of memory,

black hair braided with months of snow.
All the way down this mountain

she beseeches the dark to answer,
an orphan in the fluorescent night—

and a thread of yellow wings descend,
this day already broken from the withered year,

when she began a woman alone
and found, not looking, the sand of home.

Entre los monarcas con Marien

Esta mañana de junio fuera de la cañada
de lengua y país, la conduzco

al aeropuerto donde agrupados
en la espuma de manos que la guiaron hasta la preparatoria

en la salvia y piedra americana—
la luz de la pista levanta sus ojos

a través de las fronteras de hueso y maíz
hasta un pueblo de hermanas en el mojado de mosquito.

Como Lawrence en un campo de sol e indios,
se va hasta la costa verde de memoria,

pelo negro trenzado con meses de nieve.
Por todo la bajada de esta montaña

suplica la oscuridad para una respuesta,
una huérfana en la noche fluorescente—

y un hilo de alas amarillas descende,
este día ya quebrado del año seco,

cuando comenzó mujer sóla
y encontró, sin buscar, la arena del hogar.

At the Legislative Hearing on Mental Health Cuts

When the hearing is over, I drive
into the wilderness of sage, my tent
                              close at hand—
my pickax at the ready, turn at last
to thread my small town and know
very little will change—save the bruised

fingers of those who serve, those who
heal what is left of the arm, the body
                              that wanted more
than dust and doubt at the podium,
would have settled for a month of snow
without the dressing of kindness,

the perennial kiss of make-do, before
                              the sever of bone.

The Labyrinth of a Mind

for Carolyn Kizer

Now you are truly in the hands of the dispossessed,
nursed into numbness by women half your age, nursed

into the holy land you wrote of your late friend, Hayden.

This subterfuge, this dying of a mind, is not holy,
and it does not want to be such. Your eyes

turn to what they need in this room: the poems
read over and over. And you descend their depths.

I had few teachers. One was you—on that couch

in Mountain View, reading word by word the first book,
written in the catacombs of grad school. Do we ever finish,

this thirty-year interlude with you in the eucalyptus grove
and I on my stone perch in the mountains, do we ever

arc the silence of a mind? You have no strength

to dredge the life-blows, and yet this day returns
to the subtle relief of hours together, the diapason

of poetry remembered. This is our truth,
our refuge, our shared, spoken gravity.

These are Old Windows

I.

They have seen stars
and men hobbled to stones
below their feet, bent
to the truck bed with bricks
and mortar for the walls
that rise to glass shards.

These windows with wood frames
watch the moon give
itself to lovers
with a cigarette
afloat in the smoke
of the Albayzín—

These windows have marched
to the graves of poets, stood erect
with morning glories and
wisteria on the panes,
a thin relief of history
outside the house.

These windows have closed out
two centuries of dust and cold
and lies to frame the sun,
a cloud, and dying moon
like Borges, whose eyes
were serpents.

II.

These windows salute
with reflection,
they have no paint
beneath the surface.
They cannot hide from the banal.
They retrieve the day as it falls—

In the morning paper, an Iraqi woman
tears at her dress, her breasts
blind with grief at the loss of her son
in the bed of a truck for stones
that could have been here:
this street, this son, this stone.

And the sons will read other stories
in the window when they rise
to salute the chosen,
and the stones fall
to the patio of orange brick
and a church, and a window.

And whether Christ or Allah
in the glass, the shard of belief
guides the moon to shore in the west,
and the sons to home in the east,
and the brief hours of a flower
open the wooden cheekbones again.

My Brother, Afloat at Sea

You call with the news of a broken rudder—
a cheap part, wire money, but is it really
the rudder—no less a part of you than us,
your dockside kin, this hull that barely hoists
a makeshift sail, the sad cabin of wrenches
and diesel fumes, what slips away with the absence
of a mooring in low tide and high, the lazy squall
of seagulls and cormorants that serve as memory
of this time, floating to the anchorage of another,
what you receive for the trade of labor, the skiff
of little worry save the intermittent cables
to stave the brine of wearing to nothing
but drifting from shore, my brother,
abraded, in the solace of storms.

Mass in La Granita for Tita's Ninetieth

If you believe a woman of ninety
      prays to a God women may know,
and if the rain seeps beyond

      her pores to those who sweat
          the pews, her eight children and
theirs who rollick the humid sun,

      if the tumult that sweeps this land
          calms in the reading of scripture,
then you will know her:

tumbler of thanks, a meter of grace
      on this Central American soil,
what steels the tribe of women

      who belong to more than volcanoes
          and labor—this matriarch who
depends on the wet upheaval.

The Bus to Ajijic

On this Saturday before Easter
she sits next to me with her
infant daughter, virgin
of the overcrowded bus, descendant
of the maternal goodness
that looms in her partly crossed eyes,

and the nineteen–year-old begs her to quiet
because I cannot stop staring
into their threshold of peace,
and from the front, a woman
twists in the aisle of shoulders, a face
once at the breast of a mother

without supposition and fear
to follow the harvest of men,
and she acknowledges the child
at my side, the braids at my arm,
and whispers to our mutual assignation:
the carnal years passed from woman to man

in this small universe of mother
and infant who rise to leave
in the swarm of hats and hands,
spent in the jacaranda overhead.

Red Rock, Downpour

Red rock, globe mallow, rain thrum.
Up the creek bed to paintbrush.

Last night I studied literature
in a Reno hospital, and today,

in the southern desert of Pahrump,
dissect hunger in a church:

who will eat from the easy chair,
who from the iodine street?

And the echo of rock, up-canyon,
released from what stone mouth?

A wren in the juniper serves note
after note to the wind: no bird like this.

In the hospital, in the church. The yucca
pretends not to notice. How many

walk this sand to redeem
the outline of a face? When the red fingers

of dust begin to grieve, I turn to home,
the candle lit for sudden arrival.

Words

Would that any word wake America
from its slumber, I would surrender all hope
of writing another poem and join hands in its offering.

About the Author

Shaun T. Griffin has dedicated his life to creating a caring community. In 1991, he and his wife, Deborah, founded Community Chest, a nonprofit organization that directs more than thirty programs for northern Nevada including hunger relief, service learning, emergency shelter, drug and alcohol counseling, early childhood education, and art and social justice projects (he retired in 2017). Throughout this time he has taught a poetry workshop at Northern Nevada Correctional Center and published a journal of their work, *Razor Wire*. *Because the Light Will Not Forgive Me—Essays from a Poet*, was published by the University of Nevada Press in 2019. Southern Utah University Press released *Anthem for a Burnished Land*, a memoir, in 2016. He edited *From Sorrow's Well—The Poetry of Hayden Carruth*, published by the University of Michigan Press in 2013. *This Is What the Desert Surrenders, New and Selected Poems*, came out from Black Rock Press in 2012. In 2014 he was inducted into the Nevada Writers Hall of Fame, and in 2006, he received the Rosemary MacMillan Award for Lifetime Achievement in the Arts. For over three decades, he and his wife have lived in Virginia City in the shadow of novelist, Walter Van Tilburg Clark's, former house.

CPSIA information can be obtained
at www.ICGtesting.com
Printed in the USA
FSHW011253050320
67845FS